# Utility Solutions for Businesses

Small and Medium Enterprises

By Cherry-Ann Carmelia Craigwell

## About the Author

Cherry-Ann Craigwell is a consultant on commerce and business development. She has 27 years experience in Customer Service, Business and Process Development, Strategic Management and Business Culture Management. Her experience has shown there is the need for Small and Medium Enterprises to adopt fundamental practices to support their sustainability and competitiveness in the environment. Her passion for building business has purposed her to provide operational and strategy coaching services to Sole Traders and Small and Medium Sized Enterprises.

Other books written by the author –

The Building Ideas Guide Handbook

U.S.B. – Utility Solutions for Businesses – Small and Medium Enterprises Copyright © 2021 by Cherry-Ann Carmelia Craigwell. All rights reserved. Printed in the United States of America. No part of this book may be reproduced in any manner whatsoever without permission except in the case of brief quotation embodied in critical articles and reviews.

ISBN 9798745932755

# Table of Contents

Introduction .................................................................... 5
Small and Medium Enterprises Advantages ...................... 6
Understanding Opportunity ............................................... 7
Product / Service – Market Relationship ........................... 10
Resource Management ..................................................... 11
Inspiration vs. Discipline .................................................... 13
Summary ............................................................................ 14
Understanding the Environment ........................................ 16
Your Market, Your Customer ............................................. 18
Industry .............................................................................. 19
Networking ......................................................................... 21
Competition ........................................................................ 22
Social Responsibility ........................................................... 23
Summary ............................................................................ 25
Market Visibility ................................................................. 27
Summary ............................................................................ 30
Management ...................................................................... 31
Product Life Cycle ............................................................... 33
Resource Management ...................................................... 36
Finance Management ........................................................ 37
Multiples of Two Law ......................................................... 39

| | |
|---|---|
| Start –up | 39 |
| Self Sufficiency | 40 |
| Operation Management – Maintenance | 41 |
| Expertise | 42 |
| Communication Channels and Information | 44 |
| Logistics | 45 |
| Physical Assets | 45 |
| Passive Income | 46 |
| Summary | 47 |
| Strategy Management | 49 |
| Summary | 51 |
| Appendices | 52 |
| Pestel Diagram | 53 |
| Products / Service Element Checklist | 54 |
| Maintenance Checklist Sample | 55 |
| Pricing Guide | 56 |
| Creativity and Accountability Card | 57 |

# Introduction

Success lies in good health. A healthy body, mind and environment lead to a successful life. One can control the body and the mind and with consistent effort, impact their environment.

Your organization as the name implies, is an organism, it requires a healthy body - the operatives of the business; a healthy mind – the strategies and planned actions; and the environment which consists of your market, industry, network and society.

The Utility Solutions for Businesses (USB) – SME'S considers what the challenges Small and Medium Enterprises experiences and, what are some of the measures that can be employed to negate the effects the environment may have on the business and with consistent effort how it can positively impact the environment.

For anything to be effective it requires application and consistency. The USB has templates that can be easily adapted for application within the business.

A healthy business attracts investor confidence, easy access to finance, exhibits innovation and stability.

Plug in your USB and witness the difference.

# Small and Medium Enterprises Advantages

Knowing where your business has the advantage is a good place to start to create a successful journey.

The following lists the advantages SME's have in a market. Identify which of the following you can ascribe to as your business's strengths:

- Delivery of products and services can be personalized.
- Relationship oriented communication with the environment and the market.
- Can easily adapt to environment changes through creativity.
- Better controls on product life cycle management.
- Creating market advantage by enhancing market relationship is easy.
- Ability to easily develop and control internal communication systems.
- Developing and maintaining desired culture in the business is manageable.
- Implementation of processes and policies tend to be uncomplicated and effortless.

Leveraging on your identified strengths you can use them to improve on the other available advantages highlighted, which, as an SME you can naturally have.

# Understanding Opportunity

Opportunity can be derived from two different perspectives:

- From personal resources which includes expertise, qualifications, network and physical assets.
- Generated from an Idea that satisfies a need in the market.

These two perspectives will determine the type of relationship you will have with the market.

The first perspective allows for the employment of immediate resources to provide services to a market. The employment of this perspective can be tunneled vision, as the initial thought of service delivery is primarily based on what 'I' or 'the businesses have and is capable of doing. It may not necessarily consider what the market requires; actually the search for a market and market needs only begins after the initial setup of resources.

The second perspective considers what the market needs. A need is recognized and a solution is created. Resources are then acquired to implement the solution for the need that was identified in the market.

See the following infographic diagram to better explain the concept.

# UNDERSTANDING OPPORTUNITY

## COMPARING TWO PERSPECTIVES OF OPPORTUNITY

This is what I can do. Expertise, Qualifications, Network & Assets

This is what I should do. Idea that satisfies a need in the market.

| Marketing Process | Marketing Process |
|---|---|
| Resources providing services to different markets. | Solutions to a primary target market and optional secondary market. |
| **Competitive Analysis** | **Competitive Analysis** |
| Larger competition network to manage, difficult to stand out | Targeted competition network easy to differentiate. |
| **Market Visibility** | **Market Visibility** |
| A large market to gain credibility and visibility | Target market with a solution, to gain credibility and visibility |
| **Business Sustainability** | **Business Sustainability** |
| Dependant on the services that can be offered with resources | Dependant on the ability to satisfy the need in the market |

The previous infographic representation reflects where consideration of the two perspectives is done separately. We can see the limitations and danger in applying one single perspective to the purpose of the business.

The following Market Relationship Matrix highlights the four combinations that can be derived in the application of both perspectives.

## Market Relationship Matrix

|  | WHAT I CAN DO — HIGH | WHAT I CAN DO — LOW |
|---|---|---|
| **WHAT I SHOULD DO — HIGH** | * Very resourceful<br>* Good Understanding of the target market needs | * Limited resources<br>* Good Understanding of the target market needs |
| **WHAT I SHOULD DO — LOW** | * Very resourceful<br>* Little understanding of the target market needs | * Limited resources<br>* Little understanding of the target market needs |

Can you look at your business and identify which quarter your business fit in?

# Product / Service – Market Relationship

Your market is the consumers who you are targeting to offer your product / service. It is important to know exactly what the product / service must have to please the market. There are many elements to a service or a product that satisfies consumers and these are:

- Taste
- Smell
- Touch
- Sound
- Sight
- Function
- Availability
- Affordability
- Classification

The elements are combined to offer an experience to the consumer. Where a product fails to offer satisfaction in any of the elements, it creates GAPS (*Guaranteed Areas for Providing a Solution*). These GAPS offer opportunities to create ideas to make the product more satisfying to the customer.

What elements of service that your product or service satisfies the market and which elements it can be improved on?

## Resource Management

The need to have the right resources to fulfill the services in the market is critical. One must consider the business's products / services, level of expertise, location / distribution channel, communication channels / information, financial status and physical assets.

The manner in which these resources are maintained and mixed can see unnecessary losses or synergy profits. The proper usage of the business's resources guides the company in offering the best services to the market with little difficulty.

Successful Resource Management can be attained by applying continuous maintenance to:

***Product / Service*** – Enhancing the product/service life cycle.

***Expertise*** – Kaizen; continuous improvement of expertise, institutional knowledge, in the business.

***Location / Distribution Channels*** – Ensure the product/service is easily accessible to the target market.

***Communication Channels / Information*** – Be networked and stay informed on how political, economical, social, technological, environmental and legal elements affect your business and its operations.

***Finance*** – Maintain budgets, record keeping and control.

***Physical Assets*** – Employ effectively and maintain continuously.

## Inspiration vs. Discipline

All businesses would have been initiated out of an inspiration that is, the process of being mentally stimulated to do something, whether it, be out of a need or the opportunity of available resources.

Discipline is the combined energy of process and control to achieve an objective. Discipline represents the proper management of the resources of the business.

Inspiration is the seed that is planted to do something and discipline is the nutrients applied to the seed and plant so as to reap a harvest.

Inspiration and discipline once habitual in the business becomes a symbiotic relationship that supports automatic growth and development.

The application of creativity (inspiration) and resource management (discipline) will support the business in being sustained and profitable.

# Summary

### Understanding Opportunity

- Resources - What I or the business is capable of.
- Market Needs - What I should do to satisfy the GAPS in the market.

### Market Relationship Matrix

Pair the two perspective of opportunity – What I can do (Resources) and What I should do (Market Needs). It is important the business tries to maintain its position in the top left quadrant most times. This is done by always listening to the consumer/market and effectively managing your resources. (See Market Relationship Matrix pg.3)

### Product / Service – Market Relationship

Listening to your market highlights the needs which can be resolved. Some listening devices are:

    Customer Surveys

    Social Media Platforms

    Blind samples and comments exercises

    Giveaways

Using the product/service elements checklist to guide (see Appendix) and finalize your findings as to what the market needs is.

**Resource Management**

Resource Management is the commitment and continuous maintenance of the resources in the business. This is further expounded on in our chapter on Management.

The implementation of a maintenance checklist (see Appendix) can help establish the habit of maintenance for the business.

## Understanding the Environment

The Environment has a number of important components for you to utilize to support sustainability and development of your business; these will be addressed in this chapter.

Considerations will be given to:

>Your market, your customer

>Industry

>Networking

>Competition

>Social Responsibility

The eco system of your business involves the environment and the mechanisms utilized to facilitate how well you have adapted to it.

There are different elements in the environment that one should pay particular interest to, and these are:

Political – The political status of a country affects macro activities and culture energy of your environment. A democratic and free economy will be different to communist and socialist economies. Do you know the political environment in which the business exists?

Economical — Understanding the economic status of the environment or your target market is crucial to your success. This will guide you in the classification and affordability element of your product or service.

Social — The social environment will determine how well your product will be received based on trends. This element of the environment will support your marketing strategy and target market options.

Technological — Reflections on the environment technological status quo will help you determine the best way to communicate and deliver your products and services to your target market and to possibly implement cost effective technologies in the production of your product / service.

These elements are highlighted in the PESTEL diagram (Appendix) which helps you to determine what environment your business exists in.

Let us apply the elements of the environment to the five main components of the environment so as to develop the best approach in creating a rewarding relationship between the business and its environment. The components of the environment being: your customer, industry, network, competition and social responsibility.

## Your Market, Your Customer

Your market or your customer lies in society. As explained before it is your business's purpose to see a need and fill a need. In satisfying that need, you would have created a customer.

In the satisfaction of that need, your business can also create a utility product or service for that segment of society, that is, a product or service that has now become mandatory for the particular customer to have.

When identifying your market / customer one must consider the following:

      Who are my customers?

      How relevant is the need?

      What do they consider as value?

      Where are they?

The Social and Economical elements in the environment will guide you in the answers to these questions.

## Industry

An attribute of a successful business is one where it functions well in its industry. It is important to know and understand your industry standards, legal obligations, major challenges, 'tricks of the trade' and supporting associations.

Industry awareness will guide you on the trending developments and needs of the market your business serves. As a business owner you must be au current with how the regional and local economy is affecting the industry in which you are operating.

The following elements of the environment, when changed will impact industries: political, economical, social, technological, environmental and legal.

Here is an example of changes of elements and how they can impact an industry and by extension a business: *'there is a change in the Vehicle Industry via the environmental and legal elements, where legislation is passed to reduce carbon emissions through the usage of vehicles – The sale of vehicles will be impacted as dealers will be required to increase their inventory on hybrid and electric vehicles which implements a gradual reduction of fossil fuel operated vehicles.*

*As a car dealer it is important to know and source new and reputable suppliers. This will require the skill of networking and negotiating for new suppliers.*

*Through your Market Relationship with the market you will have to sensitize your target market on the changes of the elements in the vehicle industry. This can be further enhanced by providing supporting services for the new vehicle types.'*

As highlighted by the example a change in elements in one component of your environment will require the business to change its strategy so as to maintain business sustainability.

If the business can positively respond to scenarios of changes in the environment and implement roadmap strategies, these changes will support the business in its continued operations and sustainability.

## Networking

Your network is extremely important, the old adage "show me your friends and I will know the person you are" is true for personal reference as much as for business relations. A business ability to network with trusted and reliable suppliers, attract competent talent, sustain stable financial relationships and navigate value-add association with the community, creates a symbiotic relationship with the environment which allows it to deliver on its' commitment to the market.

A network will be affected by the elements of the environment and as a business it is important that you stay informed on what the current affairs are and how they affect your network.

A stable network gives the business the advantage to be sustained and opportunities to leverage for growth.

In any environment there will be constant change. It is important therefore you are aware of the potential of your network and its ability to deliver on the resources you will require ensuring continued business activity.

## Competition

"No one thing is perfect."

This is great news! It simply means that there will be GAPS in the product and services you and your competitors are offering to a market / customer.

In a society everyone is different and there will be no one product that will satisfy all persons. With that understanding it offers opportunity for you to enhance what is already on the market and by extension make better your offerings to the target market and give you the reality of capitalizing on a larger market share.

Appreciate the competitors' products and services, and using the Elements of Products and Services checklist; compare your offering to that of your competitor.

This will guide you to identify where you need to improve on the service to make it better for your target market or attractive to a new target market.

The elements to consider in this component will be Social and Environmental.

## Social Responsibility

*"There is one social responsibility of businesses, to use its' resources and engage in activities to increase profits so long as it stays within the rules of the game which is to say engages in open and free competition without deception or fraud."*

*– Milton Freidman*

The above statement addresses the basic behavior of the social responsibility of a business. Simplified as the following:

- To make a profit
- Remain competitive
- Maintain effective resource management
- Operate with integrity
- Deliver on services as committed

These are the expectations of a business.
A business is firstly responsible to ensure it functions effectively which allows for comfortable employment and sustainability, competitive market relationships and a strong financial position.

As an SME your contribution to the local economy counts and your commitment to ensuring statutory obligations are upheld and sustainable employment is met and relied on.

Management is an action oriented task and when effective it delivers on the social responsibility of your business.

Social Responsibility will be guided by the Legal and Political elements which will chart what are the requirements to be fulfilled in your social responsibility of the business. It is important that you remain updated with the regulations on labor, taxes and other statutory requirements.

# Summary

### *Your market, your customer*

Always ask and know the answers to the following questions:

- Who are my customers?
- How relevant is the need?
- What do they consider as value?
- Where are they?

### *Industry*

Always stay current with information about your industry and the different elements that affect it. Be aware of the local and regional economy and how it impacts on the industry you are operating in. Industry information is important to the continued sustainability of your business.

### *Networking*

Build a competent and reliable business network relationship with:

- *Suppliers
- *Community
- *Expertise / Talent
- *Financial Institutions
- *Relevant Trade Associations

## Competition

"No one thing is perfect."

Appreciate what the competition offers to the market, analyze the market response and offer your solutions to where the competition has left GAPS. Use the product/service elements checklist to guide you.

## Social Responsibility

As an SME your continued successful existence is important to the economy in which you operate in, as such your key social responsibilities are:

    *To make a profit
    *Remain competitive
    *Maintain effective resource management
    *Operate with integrity
    *Deliver on services as committed

## Market Visibility

Market Visibility is the phrase used that describes how well you are seen in the market. This is achieved by your marketing efforts and customer experience feedback.

Market Visibility includes your logo, tag line, advertising and your customer responses on the services of your product.

Your business can create beautiful presentations of the product / service being offered but if the customer experience do not mirror what is being offered you can get negative feedback and dissatisfied customers.

On the contrary the opposite can also happen, where you have a product / service that satisfy a need in the market excellently, but, if you do not have a strong advertising strategy or presentation you will retain loyal customers but also limit the growth of your customer base.

It is important that attention be placed on both your presentation and your customers' experience. Always improve on your presentation highlighting the difference and the advantage of your product / service and always work on improving the customer experience by providing support systems to encourage market feedback.

## Some Advertising Tools

Flyers

Coupons

Billboards

Email Blasts

Mobile Ads

Uniforms

Direct Mail

Pull Outs

Trade Shows

Websites

Social Media

**Customer Feedback Channels**

Surveys

Call Ins

Giveaways

Business App

Loyalty Program / Cards

Social Media Interaction

The combination of advertising tools such as direct mail or coupons with a customer feedback channel like a survey can lead to creating a customer loyalty base.

Market visibility supports a business in improving its products and services and helps guide how the product/service lifecycle will be affected and when.

The product/service life cycle will be addressed under our next chapter, Management.

## Summary

Market Visibility is the action of advertising and customer feedback.

The successful combination of advertising tools and customer feedback mechanisms helps to build a strong market visibility presence.

# Management

*"Management produces economic and social development with saving and capital investment"*
— Peter Drucker

The above statement highlights the importance of Management in business. It signifies effective management will lead to economic and social development allowing for savings and capital investment for the business. This is the priorities of all businesses. As such action oriented and effective management is extremely necessary.

As a business owner you are a capitalist first. You hold the means of production and resources. A reminder on these resources is as follows:

- Product / Service
- Expertise
- Location / Distribution Channel
- Communication Channels / Information
- Finance
- Physical Assets

Management assures that these resources are effectively utilized to produce economic and social development, savings and capital generation through filling a need in the market.

Action oriented management can also be termed as active maintenance.

The effective maintenance and controls of these resources can be classified under four major functions:

- Product / Service Life Cycle Management
- Operations Management – Expertise, Location/Distribution Channel, Physical Assets
- Finance Management – Maintenance of; Budget, Cash Flow, Income & Expenditure Statement and Balance Sheet, Multiples of Two law.
- Environment Management – Industry Knowledge, Communication Channels

As a capitalist it is important to produce a product / service that the market needs at a minimal cost while ensuring market visibility for increase sales. This will require efficient maintenance of your resources; the best resources mix and the adoption of building good market relationships.

Next we shall look at the Product / Service Life Cycle and the continuous management of it and why it's necessary for the product / service to remain relevant so as to ensure the continued interest of the market and sustainability of the business.

## Product Life Cycle

The understanding of your product / service life cycle is also important to the success of creating economic development, savings and capitalist growth.

The following diagram demonstrates how the product / service life cycle can be engaged.

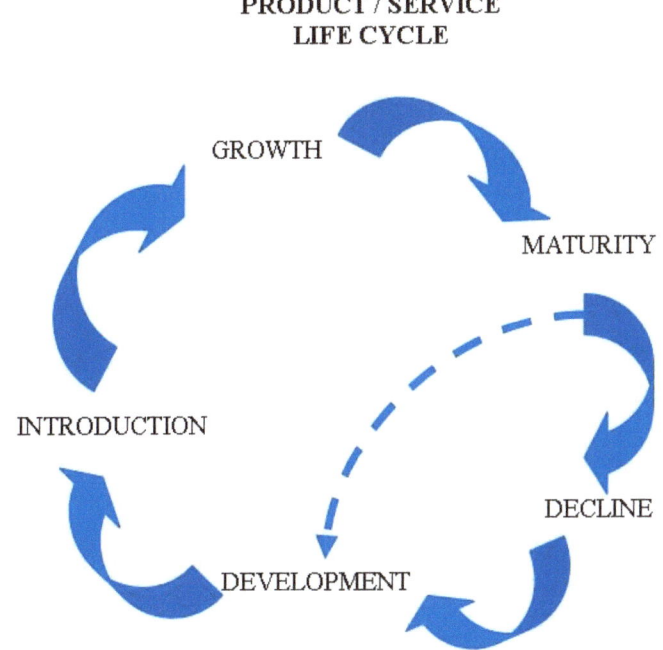

The product / service Life Cycle identifies what happens with a product or service at each stage of its existence.

The **Development** stage is the idea being invested in to make it a product / service.

The **Introduction** on the market will be supported by ensuring your presentation is seen by a wide sector of the market through effective advertising.

The **Growth** stage is at the point where the product increases in sales regularly and this is measured by the market response through sales and customer feedback.

**Maturity** identifies the maximum sales that can be achieved for this particular product that is targeted for a particular market.

If nothing is done to the product/service, the product/service will plateau and can experience a **Decline** especially if it becomes a point of competition to another.

The dashed arrow that connects **maturity** to **development** is a proactive approach the business can take to identify where there may be GAPS that can improve the solutions the product / service offers to the market and what new target markets that can be engaged in.

The term **cost benefit analysis** should be introduced at the stage of **maturity**. It is here the business should use this window to reduce the cost of production and delivery of service to maximize on the profits earned.

Depending on the product and market response, the maturity stage can be for a period that is medium to long term. Creating the best cost effective approach will require considerations to manufacturing cost, expertise cost, delivery cost, packaging cost, material cost and location cost.

Networking and negotiating skills is harnessed and use to help bring about a reduced cost of production.

As a guide cost of production should not exceed 55% of sales price.

See Appendices for pricing guide.

## Resource Management

Effective resource management is important. It is the ability to identify the usefulness in the resource and the market value it has while comparing that to the businesses needs and direction.

You should discern if the resource is effective or not. This can be easily identified with the proper maintenance and waste management policies and processes being adopted. This ensures the business acquires add value from the resource and minimizes losses and leakage.

The proper maintenance of the resource can be done through the implementation of checklists, processes and policies. Habitual use of these items helps the business function effectively. Note a checklist can be electronically prepared and used. A simple habit created develops into a process, and a policy can be a one page document guiding the expected outcome in a plan or strategy. The correct and consistent implementation of these three builds a strong and guided foundation of institutional knowledge.

As the business grows it is expected the details in the maintenance of the resources will become more thorough. This can be supported by the additional support systems from the increase of employment.

## Finance Management

Finance Management is the ability to plan, record and control the finances of the business.

The planning involves in setting a *budget*. A simple budget that will guide the amount of monies needed to cover expenses that will occur in a specific period of time and the number of sales that needs to be generated to cover those expenses. Your budget is important as it highlights key information such as:

- The least and high priced, expense items
- High and low Income earning products

This information will help you to adjust what you plan to do to ensure more profitability.


*Recording* is extremely important. Simple bookkeeping methods can be employed using accounting tools that can be found online or downloadable apps or accounting programs. They help in the recording of invoices, bills, taxes etc. paid and sales receipts made.

Every transaction must be recorded timely; *this is a critical point*; if your budget is set for a particular period transactions done in that same period must be noted for via bookkeeping. This is where you can do the comparisons for control over a specific period.

***Control*** is the ability to monitor expense and income to what you would have budgeted. This is important as it will highlight a number of things:

- Unnecessary / Missed expenses
- Excess / reduction in expenses
- Best and Least Revenue Earning product
- Market responses to products (Sales Volume)
- Profit Attained

Control guides the business to make strategic decisions on how to decrease expenses and enhance sale efficiency. Sale efficiency here will be aligned to setting attainable sales targets, monitoring sales lines, create product differentiation and engaging new local target markets, following the principles of the product / service life cycle as addressed earlier.

The need for Financial Management as in Budget, Recording and Control supports the business in knowing its financial position. The financial position is reflected in its Income and Expenditure Statement, and Balance Sheet. Income and Expenditure statement reflects expenses and income done during a period, while the balance sheet presents the value of the company. The value of the company will be the assets (property, machinery, cash, investments) being compared to liabilities, monies owed (Loans, Mortgages, Statutory payments etc.).

## Multiples of Two Law

In Finance, control is best measured by setting goals in cost, sales and profits.

The Multiples of Two Law (MTL) helps the business to habitually engage in processes to monitor cost and sales, build capital and use lean operations. Very simply it considers the least amount of profit the business should make annually.

### Start –up

As a start-up, it is challenging to record a profit at the beginning, as there will be many new entry challenges the business will experience.

The business should aim to have a loss of no more than 4% in the first year, no more than 2% loss in the second year and a *gain* of 2% in the third year.

It is advisable that the owners have a capital reserve that represents 6% of total start up budget, set aside as an emergency relief fund. (This should not be a part of any monies borrowed or considered as part of the start-up budget). This emergency relief fund will continue to support the business in the first two years of operation, giving it the opportunity to attain a profit in its third year.

## Self Sufficiency

For the business to be truly sustained and competitive it must be self-sufficient. This requires a reduction or total payoff of all start-up liabilities by the end of the fourth year. In the fourth year, the business should habitually engage in MTL, by reducing cost by 2% and increasing sales by 2%. This is a base requirement for ensuring profitability of 4% per annum. If profits are higher excellent, but one must ensure the business practices cost reduction and sales increase at all times.

Raising capital is important to be self-sufficient, and it is advisable 12% of gross profits from sales are capital investment. Remaining profits are usually net off to cover other expenses and statutory liabilities.

## Operation Management – Maintenance

*"Continuous maintenance allows for the best performance of an asset"*

Developing the mindset and habit of continuous maintenance in your operations makes it easy for this particular need to be exercised regularly. Note your assets are utilized to create a product / service to generate revenue.

Assets that must be maintained are;

- Expertise – Institutional Knowledge, Career Knowledge and Leadership skills
- Communication – Communication channels and Information
- Logistics – Location and Distribution Channels
- Physical Assets – Machinery, Furniture

Each of your assets is important to the effective production of your service / product. If there is a fault in any of the assets it can cause unnecessary financial, time and quality issues in production and may even cause wastage.

### Expertise

There are three knowledge areas that must be engaged in and supported for the successful management of the expertise in your business. These are Institutional, Career and Leadership.

***Institutional Knowledge***: This knowledge is the term that states, 'This is how we do things around here'. This knowledge is instilled by the implementation of checklists, recorded processes and policies. Continuous in-house or hands on training and accountability of institutional knowledge becomes necessary for the business to ensure sustainability and continuity of its services and products without unnecessary 'employee fault' expenses.

***Career Knowledge***: Career Knowledge is the improvement of the individual's understanding and knowledge of information and standards in the career they have chosen. It applies to specialized positions and jobs such as Engineering, Accounting, Medicinal, Culinary and many more. The business should encourage persons requiring technical skills, for the production of its product / service, to be au current in value.

***Leadership Knowledge***: 'Leaders are not necessarily born, they can be made'. A leader is someone who can easily get the job done with the support of other team members. They motivate positively and are comfortable to hold persons accountable to ensure deadlines and quality productivity is met.

Expertise Maintenance also includes the business's approved accountability process, such as periodic appraisals, which must be upheld to ensure that all persons are operating efficiently in institutional knowledge, career knowledge and leadership knowledge. The accountability measures are very important as the business wants to ensure that it is getting value for money from its human resources.

Accountability measures must always be noted in documents such as meeting notes, training sessions, disciplinary meetings and periodic appraisals.

## Communication Channels and Information

The maintenance of a proper communication channel is extremely important for the free flow of relevant and valuable information.

A line of communication can be established via email, online group chats, Team Apps, internal memorandums or regular meetings. Once established and kept active it will inhibit the recognition of the informal communication channel that all businesses tend to develop.

If the business lacks a formal and approved line of communication it will leave for the development of an unmanaged and confused one which can result in the disastrous efforts of false news and damaging reports.

Communication maintenance is extremely important for the development of the culture of the business.

The business must also stay current with information about its environment, industry, market and internal situation. This is readily needed to make informed decisions on production, marketing and business strategy.

## Logistics

Logistics here is the commercial activity of transporting goods to customers. The platform in which the customer receives the product / service is important. It may be done via vehicle delivery, a retail store shelf or at the business's location e.g. fast food or personal services. The maintenance of this platform is important and each has its dimension in providing the best for the market.

Vehicle delivery requires the courtesy of the delivery personnel, proper maintenance of the vehicles and excellent traffic time management. A retail store shelf will require continuous presence of the product on the shelves, consumer friendly and attractive packaging and consistency in volume.

Location for the serving of a product / service must be hygienic and outfitted to the service being offered.

## Physical Assets

The proper maintenance of Physical Assets can be successfully engaged in by actively using a checklist; this will guide the business in periodic maintenance and relevant services required. Please note the cost of maintenance for assets must be included in your overhead costs. Periodic servicing and maintenance ensures your assets can continue to operate efficiently.

## Passive Income

As quoted prior engaging in successful resource management will see savings and economic growth in the business.

This allows for the business to invest in other instruments that will add value to the business's growth and development.

Creating streams of passive income supports the business in achieving its financial goals. Some passive income generators are:

- Property / Machinery Rental
- Purchase of Stocks and Shares
- Purchase of Government Bonds
- Purchase of Equity Bonds

Diversifying the services the business offers also can create passive income streams for the business, these are:

- Franchising
- Private Label Products / Services
- Create an App
- Create an online Course
- Engage in Ecommerce

It is advisable that the business create wealth through the employment of more than one income streams.

# Summary

**Product Life Cycle Management**

Management of the Product Life Cycle ensures the products and services offered by the business remains relevant to the target market. It also guides the business in monitoring cost and production sustainability. The proper management of the product life cycle allows for product and service longevity, increase market visibility and sustained sales.

**Resource Management**

This covers all the resources of the business:

    Finance Management

    Operations Management

    Expertise Management

    Communications Management

    Logistics Management

    Physical Management

The effective maintenance of the resources of the business is important to ensure the continued efficiency and expected results in performance of the resource. The easy implementation of checklists, processes and policies help with the development of institutional knowledge, easy performance measurement tools, accountability frameworks and proper waste management practices. It is important the business is habitual in its maintenance practices as it saves the business from experiencing leakages in time, finance, and quality.

**Passive Income**

It is important that the business considers other measures to create a passive income line. This means that there is another means of income that is derived without the use of continuous high-cost resources.

## Strategy Management

Strategy is the employment of careful and practical thought in creating a blueprint to achieve an objective. Management is the process of the implementation of the blue print and accountability of achieving the objective. Strategy Management therefore must be an accountable implementation of creativity and must be engaged for both short and long term objectives of the business.

Short term objectives can focus:

- on the best options for resources utilization
- maintenance of suppliers and inventory
- on product / service life cycle management
- ongoing market relationship
- employee engagement
- on controlling operation cost

Long term objectives that can be considered:

- Increasing revenue streams
- Backward and Forward Integration
- Targeting new markets
- Capital Investments

Strategies can either be categorized as Operational or Transformational. The application of an operational strategy will be as indicated to the continuous operations of the business:

An example of an operational strategy is a fast food outlet introducing a new combo on their menu that fits a family.

When the business is habitual in applying strategy management to its short term objectives it ensures sustainability of the business. Sustainability must be a daily objective of the business.

A transformational strategy is one that is adopted that will change the operations of the business; an example of a transformational strategy is a fast food retail outlet adopting a franchise brand.

The employment of strategy management on its Long term objectives allows the element of growth to be experienced by the business.

For the continued success of the business creativity and accountability must be habitually engaged in its operations. As a capitalist the business must utilize its resources to generate savings and investment, while holding themselves accountable for doing such.

In the appendices there is a tool to support creativity and accountability actions.

## Summary

The thought energies for planning and action to be adopted by your business is necessary to sustain the daily operations, short term objectives, long term objectives and transformational decisions.

The application of strategy is important and must be enshrined in the accountable operations of the business.

Knowing your strengths, the environment and your goals will help the business develop the roadmaps to accomplish its objectives.

# Appendices

- PESTEL Factors diagram
- Product / Services Elements Checklists
- Sample Maintenance Checklist
- Price Guide
- Creativity and Accountability Action Card

# Pestel Diagram

Businesstoyou.com—Scanning the environment PESTEL Analysis—http://www.business-to-you.com/scanning-the-environment-pestel-analysis, 18/09/2016

## Products / Service Element Checklist

| Idea Element | Existing Idea | My Idea |
|---|---|---|
| Taste | ○ ○ ○ ○ ○<br>1 2 3 4 5 | ○ ○ ○ ○ ○<br>1 2 3 4 5 |
| Smell | ○ ○ ○ ○ ○<br>1 2 3 4 5 | ○ ○ ○ ○ ○<br>1 2 3 4 5 |
| Touch | ○ ○ ○ ○ ○<br>1 2 3 4 5 | ○ ○ ○ ○ ○<br>1 2 3 4 5 |
| Sight | ○ ○ ○ ○ ○<br>1 2 3 4 5 | ○ ○ ○ ○ ○<br>1 2 3 4 5 |
| Sound | ○ ○ ○ ○ ○<br>1 2 3 4 5 | ○ ○ ○ ○ ○<br>1 2 3 4 5 |
| Function | ○ ○ ○ ○ ○<br>1 2 3 4 5 | ○ ○ ○ ○ ○<br>1 2 3 4 5 |
| Affordability | ○ ○ ○ ○ ○<br>1 2 3 4 5 | ○ ○ ○ ○ ○<br>1 2 3 4 5 |
| Availability | ○ ○ ○ ○ ○<br>1 2 3 4 5 | ○ ○ ○ ○ ○<br>1 2 3 4 5 |
| Safety / Health | ○ ○ ○ ○ ○<br>1 2 3 4 5 | ○ ○ ○ ○ ○<br>1 2 3 4 5 |
| Classification | Luxury ○<br>FMCGS ○ | Luxury ○<br>FMCGS ○ |

## Maintenance Checklist Sample

| | | Monthly Maintenance Checklist | Date Completed |
|---|---|---|---|
| Product / Service | 1 | Manage stages of product life cycle | |
| | 2 | Market visibilty monthly initiative | |
| | 3 | Monthly networking event | |
| | 4 | Update Environment (Industry) information | |
| Expertise | 1 | Host periodic meetings weekly/monthly | |
| | 2 | Prepare anniversary performance appraisals | |
| | 3 | Expertise Audit | |
| | 4 | Identify Institutional Knowledge training needs | |
| | 5 | Identify Career Knowledge training needs | |
| | 6 | Identify Leaderhsip Skills training needs | |
| | 7 | Host training sessions | |
| Logistics / Communication | 1 | Fleet Management | |
| | 2 | Facilities Management | |
| | 3 | Product packaging and distribution monitoring | |
| | 4 | Shelf product expiration monitoring | |
| | 5 | Communication of Organization Information updates | |
| Physical Assets | 1 | Ensure machinery is cleaned and serviced periodically | |
| | 2 | Ensure furnishings are safe and compliant to legal standards | |

# Pricing Guide

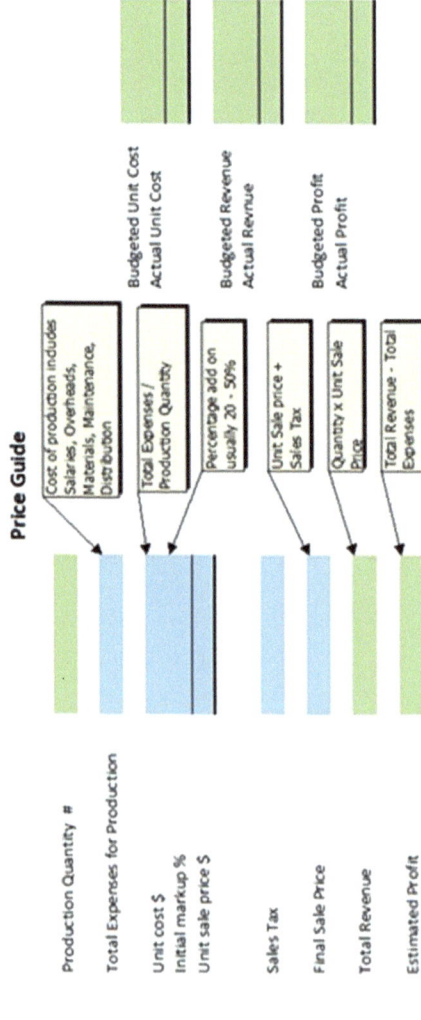

# Creativity and Accountability Card

**IDEA**
................................................................
................................................................
................................................................
**DATE**........................................................
**CREATOR NAME**:...............................................

**ACTION TEAM MEMBERS**
**NAME**              **RESPONSIBILTY**           **DEPT**
................................................................
................................................................
................................................................
................................................................
................................................................

**RESPONSIBILITY**          **TEAM MEMBER**          **DUE DATE**
................................................................
................................................................
................................................................
................................................................
................................................................
................................................................
................................................................
................................................................
................................................................
................................................................
................................................................
................................................................
................................................................
................................................................
................................................................
..........................................
**IMPLEMENTATION DATE**,,,,,,,,,,,,,,,,,,,,,,,,,,,,,,,,,,,,,,,,,,,,,,,,,,,,,,,
**SIGN OFF** ...................................................
Remember to keep tasks and responsibilities simple